Paper Mache:

The Ultimate Guide to Learning How to Make Paper Mache Sculptures, Animals, Wildlife and More!

Copyright © 2015

All rights reserved. No part of this book may be reproduced in any form without permission in writing from the author. Reviewers may quote brief passages in reviews.

Disclaimer

No part of this publication may be reproduced or transmitted in any form or by any means, mechanical or electronic, including photocopying or recording, or by any information storage and retrieval system, or transmitted by email without permission in writing from the publisher.

While all attempts and efforts have been made to verify the information held within this publication, neither the author nor the publisher assumes any responsibility for errors, omissions, or opposing interpretations of the content herein.

This book is for entertainment purposes only. The views expressed are those of the author alone, and should not be taken as expert instruction or commands. The reader of this book is responsible for his or her own actions when it comes to reading the book.

Adherence to all applicable laws and regulations, including international, federal, state, and local governing professional licensing, business practices, advertising, and all other aspects of doing business in the US, Canada, or any other jurisdiction is the sole responsibility of the purchaser or reader.

Neither the author nor the publisher assumes any responsibility or liability whatsoever on the behalf of the purchaser or reader of these materials.

Any received slight of any individual or organization is purely unintentional.

Table of Contents

Introduction

Chapter 1: The Tools of the Trade

Chapter 2 Paper Mache Animals

Chapter 3 Bug Paper Mache Models

Chapter 4: How to Make a Mask and Piñata

Conclusion

Bonus Chapter: Learn to Make Jewelry Making Bracelets and Necklaces:

Introduction

First and foremost I want to thank you for downloading the book, "The Ultimate Guide to Learning How to Make Paper Mache Sculptures, Animals, Masks, Wildlife and Much Much More!"

The art of paper mache is a fun and inexpensive activity to carry out with your friends and family, and especially with your children. It is also a great way to express your inner creativity. This type of art allows you to let your imagination run rampant while getting messy with glue and paper.

You do not have to have artistic skill on par with Picasso or Michelangelo to be able to participate in this variant of art. Paper mache is friendly towards those who feel like they don't have an artistic bone in their body. It's not about creating magnificent sculptures that result in people gaping in awe rather it is about having fun and letting your imagination run wild. If your paper mache dog looks more like a cow then so be it. It's your dog-cow hybrid thing that you made with your own two hands and you should be proud of it and not shamefully hide it in the darkest dwellings of your closet.

Thanks again for downloading this book and I hope you enjoy it!

Chapter 1: The Tools of the Trade: Everything you need to know in order to get started.

Before we get into paper mache, it would properly be a good idea to actually know what paper mache actually is about. The word paper mache roughly means chewed paper in French. This is fitting as the substances you work with do occasionally resemble mashed up paper. Paper mache can be summarized as the act of combining paper and paste or flour and using these two basic substances to create unique and cool looking figurines. This type of craft has quite a long history, with its basic mechanisms being used in hundreds of years ago in China in the formation of helmets and with the process eventually spreading to Europe where it was practiced in France and England in the 17-19th centuries in the making of wares. You too can celebrate this historic craft by making your own paper mache figures and products. In the first chapter, we will kick things off by gifting you with the tools of the trade. We will list the necessary equipment that every good paper mache novice should be familiar with and also the two chief methods used during a typical paper mache session.

Paper mache is an inexpensive and simple activity, so you will not have a lengthy list of items you will need to purchase or a whole host of jargon and complicated instructions that you will need to memorize. There are only a few items needed and a couple of pieces of valuable information to be aware of before setting out on your paper mache adventure.

This is the great thing about this type of craft; you don't have to have immense art skill or be a Picasso facsimile or have a whole array of expensive art equipment. You just need a pair of hands, a rich imagination and a few inexpensive and easily obtainable items.

Equipment

This is a list of the equipment you will need in order to paper mache.

- **Paper:** This is usually in the form of newspaper, but you could also use magazine paper, tissue paper or just plain white computer paper. It is basically up to you and your particular preferences. But just be aware that some paper will be hardier than others, for example, tissue paper will be quite hard to use and properly will not form a stable foundation. The paper that you decide upon will need to be ripped up into long strips. This is what you will use to create your paper mache masterpiece.

- **A bowl:** This is what you will use to mix your paste or flour mixture.

- **Glue or flour mixture:** Similar to the paper, what you decide to use as your adhesive substance depends upon you. For the glue mixture, you will need to mix a portion of 2/3 white glue with 1/3 cold water in a clean bowl. This mixture will need to be stirred thoroughly until the consistency is to your preferences. However, it should not be too thick. Others prefer to use the flour method. The flour concoction can be made by placing a cup of flour in a clean bowl. Into this flour, cold water should be carefully and slowly poured until it has reached a consistency that is preferable. If it is too thick add more water and if it is too runny add a few more teaspoons of flour. There should be no lumps in your flour mixture, so make sure to stir quite vigorously. Both of these adhesive methods work well and again it is up to personal preference.

- **Paint and a paintbrush**: Paint will be needed when it is time to decorate your paper mache creation. You don't want a newspaper themed dog or pig, rather you want an eye-catching and captivating pink pig or spotty dog. Paint makes your creation just a little bit more special.

- **An extra paintbrush:** This extra paintbrush will be needed in order to mix the glue or flour mix.

- **A balloon:** An inflated balloon is often used for the foundation—what the paper is glued upon to create the paper mache figure. Once the structure has been made, the balloon is simply popped. Other foundation items can also be used, such as a specific cardboard shape.

- **Your creativity:** This is properly the most vital piece of equipment needed for this project and thankfully you don't have to go too far to find it----you already have it lying in wait internally. The process of creating a paper mache sculpture is not supposed to be a chore nor a mechanical process where you methodically put pieces of paper onto the surface of a balloon with a somber expression on your face. This is supposed to be enjoyable. So remember to have fun while doing this and use your imagination when creating your pieces.

The methods

There are two chief methods that can be used when paper mache, firstly the paper/glue method and secondary, the pulp method.

Paper/glue: The paper and glue method is what is traditionally used for the bulk of the paper mache process. This is what creates the broad foundations of your creations using glue and strips of newspaper which are stuck on a balloon or other base item.

Paper mâché is quite an easy activity to carry out. Detailed below is the complete paper mâché process, from start to finish. This will hopefully make the whole process easier.

1. Make your glue or flour paste. Set this aside for the moment.

2. Next, tear up newspaper into long strips. There should be a decent amount of newspaper used as you will properly require a bit.

3. When you have your two main components sorted out, the paste and the newspaper, you can begin to paper mâché.

4. Dip a strip of newspaper into the paste and stick in onto your foundation. Complete the process until every bit of the surface is covered. You should aim to do several layers of paper mâché so that it is stable and not flimsy. After each layer, allow time for it to dry. If you wish for a blank and clear surface to paint over, you should make the final layer with white computer paper.

Pulp Method: The pulp method is used for the more delicate and intricate aspects of your sculpture. So when you have a section that needs a gentler touch, the pulp method would properly be favored over the glue/paper technique. This method involves making a pulp that is then spread over the paper mache form. Below we have listed a series of instructions on how to make this pulp:

Tear newspaper up into small pieces. These pieces shouldn't be too large or minuscule in size. They should be around 2-3 cm in length and width.

1. Place these pieces of newspaper into a bowl and pour hot water over them. All the newspaper should be covered with water. Leave to soak for a couple of hours or overnight if possible.

2. Once it has finished soaking, get your fingers into this mixture. Play around with it---squeezing, stirring and mushing it until it resembles a soggy mush of paper. There should be no lumps. If there is add more water to the mix and stir until it is lump free.

3. Add a pinch of salt. This is to make sure that it does not glob together. And then mix once more.

4. Next grab handfuls of this squashy mix and squeeze out any excess water over the sink. Return the drier pulp back to the bowl.

5. Lastly, add a few tablespoons of white glue to this mix and stir. A pulp has now been created which you can use while you

paper mache. This mix can be stored for a few days in the fridge in an airtight container.

For both of these methods, it is important that you lay newspaper out on your working surface. You should also wear old clothes that you don't mind getting messy because paper mache is a messy business!

Chapter 2: Learn how to create paper mache animals

This world is packed with lovely and charming animal friends. Some are scaly while others are fluffy; some are great while others are miniature and lastly some are adorable while others are downright unusual looking. The animal kingdom is a diverse and wild place but more than likely you properly have a favorite animal. Paper mache is a great way to celebrate your love of animals, pay homage to your favorite species of animal as well as crafting a cute little friend for your home.

In this chapter, we have presented simple and easy to follow instructions on how to make four different types of animals using the paper mache method.

A bouncy paper mache bunny

A paper mache bunny rabbit is really easy to make as well as being extremely cute. This would be a great project to do with your children around Easter or whenever you feel like making a cutesy bunny.

So go hop to it!

The equipment

- One balloon
- Quite a bit of newspaper. This should be torn into long strips ready to be used in your paper mache activities.
- Glue or flour mixture
- Some plain cardboard. This should not be too stiff or too flimsy.

- 1 cup of sand
- A funnel
- Paint
- Paintbrushes
- Decorations to adorn your bunny with. This can include googly eyes, pipe cleaners, cotton balls or pompoms and glitter.
- Felt tips
- Scissors
- Tape

The instructions

1. Blow up your balloon. Paper mache* over this foundation with at least 3-4 separate layers. Leave to dry after each layer.

2. Wait until this has hardened and then pop the balloon at the bottom. Cut a small hole into the bottom of the structure. This hole should not be too large, just big enough for a funnel to fit into.

3. Place a funnel so that it leads inside the paper mache balloon shaped structure. Pour 1 cup of sand into it using this funnel and the remove it. Place the foundation upside down so the sand does not escape.

4. Using the cardboard cutout some decorations for your little bunny. This should include some ears, large thumping feet and paws.

5. Using the tape, attach these parts in their respective places. Your bunny now should be looking less like a paper balloon and more like an actual bunny rabbit.

6. We will know paper mache over the messy areas, so the hole you used for the funnel and the spots where tape is visible. Allow this to harden once more.

7. Once there is no more wet paper-glue, it is time to make your bunny pretty. Using the paint, decorate your bunny with any color that you wish. You could have a traditional white or black bunny or a wild pink or blue bunny. It is completely up to you. After you have finished painting, allow the paint to dry. Once dry, draw black lines onto the paws.

8. Now it's time for the last of the decorations. Using glue, paste on the eyes, whiskers [use the pipe cleaners] and a nose and tail [using the pompoms].

9. And there you have it, a bunny rabbit.

Let's chill and make a penguin

Who doesn't love penguins? They are definitely one of the cuter members of the animal kingdom with their little wings and clumsy waddling walk.

Well, now you can make your very own little charming arctic friend, using the following instructions.

The equipment:

- A whole lot of torn up newspaper

- Paste
- A balloon
- Paint
- Cardboard
- Googly eyes
- A permanent marker
- Scissors
- Glue
- Glitter

The instructions:

1. Prepare your paste and newspaper. Blow up your balloon and then paper mâché over it. You should do around 2-3 layers. Leave this to dry, preferably overnight. You can pop the balloon once the paper mâché has dried or you can leave it to deflate naturally.

2. Using cardboard, cut out feet, wing,s and a beak. Paint the beak yellow or orange and then attach these to the body of your penguin, using tape. Paper mâché over this tape and the hole left by the balloon and then allow this to again dry.

3. Once everything is dry, it's time to start decorating. Paint your penguin any color you wish, stay with black and white if you wish for a traditional looking penguin. Otherwise, go crazy with any color that takes your fancy.

4. Allow the paint to dry. Once it is dry, glue on the eyes, define the feet and wings using the marker and your happy little penguin should be complete.

Old McDonald had a pig

Pigs definitely have the cute factor, with their wriggly tail, adorable snout, and bright pink skin. So why wouldn't you want to create your very own precious miniature pig made out of paper and paste. It will be a charming feature to add to your home or gift to a person who really loves pigs.

The equipment:

- Paste
- Torn up newspaper
- Cardboard
- A balloon
- Paint
- Googly eyes
- A pink pipe cleaner
- Tape
- A permanent marker
- Glue
- Scissors
- A paintbrush

The instructions:

1. Prepare the paste and newspaper.

2. Blow up your balloon until it is of a size that resembles a round pig body.

3. Paper mâché over this balloon. Do around 2-3 layers and then leave to dry. Remember to also leave it to dry between each layer. You should leave it for at least 6-7 hours though overnight is best. Once dry, pop the balloon.

4. Using the cardboard, cut out the ears of your pig. For the trotters, cut toilet rolls in half. When your pig is dry, attach these cardboard features using tape. Then paper mâché over the tape areas.

5. Now that you have your pig in a proper pig shape, it is time to decorate. Paint your pig any color you wish. If you want a traditional looking pig, paint it pink. If you want a wild and odd pig, paint it green or purple.

6. Once the paint is dry, draw on the snout using a marker.

7. Glue on its eyes and poke the pipe cleaner into the back of the pig. Twist this until it resembles a curly pig tail.

Mr. Yellow Fluff ball aka a baby chicken

Baby animals are always a fan favorite. There is just something about a cutesy cuddly baby critter that appeals to the senses, you just want to grab them and snuggle them to pieces. Baby chicks defiantly fit this bill being tiny balls of yellow fluff. Here we will show you how to make your very own paper mâché baby chick. This would be a great decoration for Easter or just to have around the house and confuse your poor cat.

The equipment:

- Paste

- Newspaper
- Permanent marker
- A balloon
- Paint
- Googly eyes
- Feathers
- Cardboard
- Scissors
- Glue

The instructions:

1. Prepare your paste and newspaper. Blow up your balloon and paper mâché over it. Leave this to dry, preferably overnight. When it is dry, you can pop the balloon if you wish or let it deflate naturally.

2. Cut out the chick's feet and beak using the cardboard. To make a beak, just cut out a triangle and bend it slightly and then paint it orange. For the feet just cut out triangles. Attach these to the body of your chick and then paper mâché over the tap. Your little chick is slowly forming.

3. Paint your chicken any color you wish. If you want your traditional little chick, you can paint it yellow. Make sure to paint the feet as well. Draw lines onto the feet, adding definition.

4. Glue on the eyes and some feathers to the top of its head, to make some cute little head fluff. And there you have to, a cute fluffy headed baby chick.

We have shown you how to make three cute animal paper mâché figures. But the animal kingdom is a vast and immense arena with vast multitudes of different animals to admire and chose to emulate with paper and glue. Most animals can be made with just a balloon, paint, cardboard and a few decorative aspects. Just spend some time experimenting and discovering your ownanimal creations.

Chapter 3: How to make bug paper mache models

Bugs seem to get a bad rap. High pitched screaming and expressions of horror seem to be the norm when a spider or centipede is spotted in the home. Noone really wants to cuddle with a sinister looking spider with all those spindly legs and that abundance of eyes. For most people, they just don't appeal to the senses and make you feel that feeling of "aww" you experience when you spot something cute, like a bunny or kitten. However, there are actually a number of different types of cool and beautiful bugs that you can make using the paper mache method. In this chapter, we will present you with all you need to know to create some charming and striking bug creatures, including a bumblebee and a magnificent butterfly.

A Buzzy Bumblebee

Bumblebees are definitely one of the most striking bugs around with its bold yellow and black stripes. Here we will show you how to make your very own eye-catching buzzy bee in only a few easy steps. So get buzzing along!

The equipment:

- A balloon
- Paper
- Paste
- Paint- yellow & black for a traditional look
- Pom-poms
- Pipe cleaners
- Glitter
- Google eyes
- Glitter
- Cardboard

- Glue
- Scissors
- Tape
- Black paper

The instructions:

1. First mix up your paste and tear up your newspaper. Next blow up your balloon and paper mâché over it. You should aim to do at least 2-3 separate layers. Once you have covered the whole balloon, leave it to dry for at least 4-5 hours but preferably overnight.

2. Once dry, pop the balloon if you wish otherwise leave it how it is. Using the cardboard, you should now cut out some wings for your bumblebee. These should be quite large; you don't want your bee to look odd with a big body and tiny wings. Attach these wings to the body using tape. Using the black paper, you should cut out a small narrow triangle. This gives your bee its painful and frightening weapon, the stinger.

3. Paper mâché over the tape areas as well as the hole left over by the balloon.

4. Now it is time to give your bumblebee a splash of color by painting him or her. If you wish to stick with a traditional looking bee, you should use black and yellow paint. With these two paint colors, paint striking stripes onto the body of the bee.

5. Your bee is starting to truly look like a bee. Now there are only a few little minor details to attend to. At present, your buzzy bee is flying blind so you need to gift it with some eyes. You can do this is in one of two ways, first you can simply glue some googled eyes onto the

little fella. Another way to add eyes would be to grab two white pom-poms, draw a pupil in the center and then glue them onto the bee. The last thing you need to add is some antennas. You can make these by poking two pipe cleaners through the front of its head. And there you have it, a cute buzzy bee. If you want to make a real special little bee, you could sprinkle glitter onto him or her making for a sparkly eye-catching piece.

A Delicate Ladybug

The ladybug is properly the most elegant and well, ladylike, bug around. There is something very bewitching and appealing about its red and black shell. Having a paper mache version in your home or room will look striking and add a vivid splash of color to your decor.

The equipment:

- A cheap plastic bowl.
- Paper
- Paste
- Paint- Red and Black if you want a traditional looking lady bug.
- Pipe cleaners
- Glitter
- Google eyes
- Glitter

- Cardboard
- Glue
- Scissors
- Tape
- Black paper

The instructions:

1. Prepare your paste mix as well as your newspaper. Get your cheap plastic bowl and paper mâché over the entire thing until there is no plastic left exposed. This includes the underside of the bowl. You have now created the foundation of your ladybug shell. Leave this to dry for at least 6 hours but preferably overnight. When this is dry, tape on six pipe cleaners to the sides, there should be three on each side. These are the legs. Next you need to paper mache over the tape areas and once again leave to dry.

2. When the whole structure is dry, it is time to start beautifying your little bug. First you need to add some color. If you want a traditional lady bug, first paint the whole figure a nice red shade. Leave this to dry. Once this layer has fully dried, it is time to add the quintessential

lady bug spots. Using black paint, paint on a number of spots onto the red base. You now have something that actually resembles a lady bug.

3. Now we are onto making the last finishing touches to your bug. So, glue the eyes on and make the antenna using glue and two pipe cleaners. Lastly, if you want a sparkly lady bug you can add some glitter. Use glue to make some patterns on the lady bug, for example a love heart or spiral, and then sprinkle some red or sliver glitter over this. And there you have it, a glittery and striking lady bug.

A Scurrying Spider

The truth of the matter seems to be that spiders are creepy and pretty unlikeable creatures. They lurk in showers and on ceilings, a monstrous horror that causes many to scream and scramble out of its proximity. Spiders are generally quite scary and sometimes the protagonist of your nightmares. For example, watching a spider devour its latest web ensconced victim is just plain disturbing. But a paper mache spider is harmless and can even be considered kind of cute in a creepy kind of way. Furthermore, a paper mache spider would be a great decoration choice for Halloween.

The equipment:
- Paste
- Torn up paper
- Two balloons
- Paint

- Paint brush
- Pipe cleaners
- Goggly eyes
- Red and white paper
- Scissors
- Craft glue

The instructions:

1. Prepare the paste and paper. Blow up one of the balloons to a reasonably large size. Paper mache over it and leave to dry. Take the second balloon and blow it up, but keep it at a small size. It should be the size of an apple or orange. Paper mache over this as well and leave it to dry.
2. Once both paper mache foundations have dried, attach the smaller one to the larger one using glue. Paper mache over the seam so it looks natural. This is your spider's head and body complete.
3. Paint over the structure in any color that you wish, for example a midnight black looks quite dynamic. Once the paint is dry, you can start adding the traditional spider adornments. For the eyes, if you wish for a true spider look then make sure to glue on eight separate eyes. For the legs, attach eight pipe cleaners, four on each side. You can attach these, by poking them into the structure. Now your spider has its many legs and eyes, the last thing you need to do is give it a fang filled mouth.

4. Using the red paper, cut out an oval shape. Next, using the white paper cut out two small triangle shapes. Glue the triangles onto the red paper, and then glue the red paper onto your spider. And there you go, you have a spooky spider.

A Beautiful Butterfly

So we have just instructed you on how to make one of the creepiest creatures out there, now we will show you how to make the beauty queen of the bug world, the butterfly. There is something whimsical and graceful about butterflies. The way they seem to seamlessly glide through the air. The butterfly is the epitome of grace and beauty. Well, with a few simple ingredients you can replicate this beauty and make your very own paper mache butterfly. You should defiantly opt to hang this butterfly from the ceiling in a representation of flight, as any true butterfly should be presented in.

The equipment:

- Paste
- Torn up newspaper
- A long cardboard tube
- Scissors
- Glitter
- Paint
- Paintbrush
- Glue
- Pipe cleaners

- Cardboard of any color. This will make your butterfly's wings so chose a color that you find pretty or appealing.
- Paint brush
- Jewels and other decorations

The instructions:

1. Prepare the paste and paper. Grab your cardboard tube and stuff it with newspaper. Paper mache over this entire structure, effectively trapping in the newspaper. Leave to dry. This is the body of your butterfly.
2. Using your colored cardboard, cut out the wings of your butterfly. These should be decent sized, not too small or too large. Attach these to the body of your butterfly using tape. Next, tape on two pipe cleaners, these are the antennas. Paper mache over the places where there is tape.
3. Now it is time to start decorating. Paint over the body of the butterfly using any color that you want.
4. Using the glue proceed to make cool patterns on the wings. These could be spirals, hearts or stars. Basically anything that takes your fancy. Sprinkle glitter over the wet glue. You could also add small jewels, which you can find at a craft store. This will make your butterfly's wings very pretty and eye catching.

Chapter 4: It's time to celebrate with paper mache: How to make a mask and piñata

Do you want to stand out at a party? Well, wearing your very own paper mache mask will properly get you noticed. And it makes a good ice breaker, where you can talk about how you made the mask and the inspiration behind it.

Furthermore, homemade piñatas are normally a hit at kid's parties. Including a brightly colored figure filled with candy is sure to go down good with any kid and frankly any adult as well. And it always looks better if you put the effort in and make it yourself.

In this chapter, we have given you the instructions on how to make a basic mask and piñata design. You can modify this to your own preferences as your skill increase with this art form.

A paper mache mask

A paper mâché mask is a great piece of decorative apparel that you or your child can wear at a themed party or a Halloween celebration. With a few simple ingredients, you can create an enchanting and amazing looking mask.

The equipment:

- Newspaper- torn up
- Plain white paper-torn up
- Paste
- A gallon jug with the labels removed.

- Paint
- Paintbrush
- Decoration items, including jewels, feathers, pipe cleaners, glitter, and anything else that you wish.
- Scissors that are capable of cutting through plastic
- Glue
- Paper mache pulp

The instructions:

1. Get a clean gallon jug and cut it in half lengthwise. Take one half and turn it upside down. This will act as the foundation of your mask. Cut out two eye holes, a mouth hole and two holes on either side of the mask.
2. Next, using the newspaper paper mache over the jug until you have done 3 layers. Do not paper mache over the holes. After it has completely dried, paper mache using the plain white paper. Leave to dry completely, this should be preferably overnight.
3. Using paper mache pulp, which we described in the first chapter, make the detailed features of the mask. For example, if you are aiming for an animal mask, make ears and a nose using the pulp. Be creative during this stage.
4. Now it is time to individualize your mask through decoration.
5. The first thing that you need to do is paint the foundation. How you decide to paint it will depend on what you want your mask to look like. If you wish to make a tiger mask, you would paint it orange with black spots. If you wanted a mime mask, you would paint it white. The same goes with the adding of decorations, it

is largely up to you. Let your imagination run wild at this stage. If you want to make a bird mask, you could add feathers or for a beautiful entrancing feminine mask you could use a lot of glitter and mini jewels. Make a mask that resounds with you.

6. Once everything is decorated properly and also dry, string through an elastic string or a ribbon through the two side holes that you made earlier. This will prevent your mask from falling off.

Let's make a piñata

A piñata is always a party favorite, mainly because it involves a shower of candy and chocolate. You can purchase a ready-made one from the store or you could unleash your wild imagination and make your own using the instructions supplied below for a simple round piñata.

The equipment:

- A round balloon
- Paste mix
- Torn up newspaper
- Paint
- A paint brush
- Glitter
- Brightly colored tissue or crepe paper
- Scissors
- Glue
- Tape

- Candy for the filling

The instructions:

1. Prepare your paste and newspaper and set aside.
2. Blow up a round balloon. Paper mache over this foundation. You should aim to do around 2-3 layers.
3. Next, it is time to paint the piñata. Taking into account, that this piñata is properly going to be for a fun vibrant party it is best to paint it a dynamic and luminous color. For example, purples, reds and yellows would be a great choice.
4. After the paint has dried, it is time to make your piñata festive. First, glue on long strips of tissue or crepe paper around the span of the balloon. Carry on doing this until you have covered the entire thing.
5. Next, get more colored tissue paper and cut it until small strips. Each of these strips should be around 2cms across and 3cms lengthwise. Glue these onto your piñata, so that they are facing upwards. Only glue the top half down and leave the bottom half free. This should make a cool ruffle effect.
6. Once you have created this look all around your piñata, it is time to fill it with candy. If the balloon that you used as a foundation is still inflated, you should now pop it. Once the balloon is popped, add the candy thorough the hole made by the balloon. Cover the hole using tape.
7. Finally, tape a ribbon or string onto the end of the piñata. You will use this to string your piñata up.

8. And there you have it, a colorful round shape structure that kids [and adults] will have fun hitting with a stick in a quest for sugar.

Conclusion

So, you have reached the end of this book on the basics of paper mache. I wish to first offer you my thanks in first downloading this book and then taking the time to read it.

I hope this book was able to help you to learn the basics of paper mache as well as how to create some cool paper mache sculptures.

The next step upon successful completion of this book is to go out and practice. Utilize your imagination and own ideas when getting messy with paper and glue. Don't follow rigid instructions but have fun and make your own strange and unique constructions. The thing about paper mache is that it is supposed to be about having fun. So remember to do just that.

On a final note, if you have found delight in this book, I urge you to please take the time to share your thoughts and post a review on Amazon. It would be really welcomed!

So, goodbye, thank you and good luck on your paper mache adventure!

Bonus Chapter: Learn to Make Jewelry Making Bracelets and Necklaces:

Beautifully made necklaces and bracelets bring out ones beauty and personality. By making your own necklaces and bracelets, you will be able to express yourself to the world loudly and creatively. They are also a good way of showing your love and appreciation to the people you care about. No expensive gift can beat a handmade necklace or bracelet made with time, effort, and love. The following bracelet and necklace projects will help you make your own first ever handmade jewelry. In mastering these, you can be more creative and add more of "you" into your work.

Project # 1: The Rainbow Strip (String and Bead Necklace)

You will need the following: any stringing medium of your choice, glass or plastic beads of any size of your choice (red, orange, yellow, green, blue, indigo, and violet), blue seed beads, colorless nail polish, ruler and scissors.

First, cut the stringing medium according to your preferred length plus at least 6 inches more (for ease in tying down the stringing medium).

Second, string the beads through and follow the color pattern of rainbows. In between each bead, insert a seed bead. So, you have to string a red bead first, then a seed bead, followed by an orange bead, and so on.

Third, once your preferred length of stringing medium is filled by the beads, draw the opposite ends together and tie a basic square knot.

Finally, brush a little amount of colorless nail polish on the knot to seal it and prevent it from unraveling. Now you have your own rainbow necklace.

Project #2: Crystals in the Night (Wire and Bead Necklace)

You will need the following: round Swarovski crystals (8mm; any color), bead caps (2 for bead), chain nose pliers, jump rings, 20 gauge jewelry wires (silver), ruler, round nose pliers, and flush cutters.

First, make a bead unit (made up of a bead, two bead caps, and a short wire). To make a bead unit, cut up a piece of short wire 1.25 inches in length. Make a loop on one end of this wire, but do not close it completely. On the other end, string in a bead cap, then a bead, and followed by another bead cap. Secure the unit by making another loop at the end (also not completely closed). Make as many bead units as necessary.

Second, connect each bead unit to form your necklace. To do this, just hook one incompletely looped end of a bead unit and another unit. Using round nose pliers, close the loops completely.

Third, if the necklace has reached your desired length, set it aside and make your own hook and catch.

Lastly, attach one end with the hook and the other with the catch. Now you have your own Crystals in the Night necklace.

Project #3: Chain of Hearts (Wire Bracelet)

You will need the following: 18 gauge jewelry wire (gold), jump rings (silver), normal string or yarn, ruler, flush cutter, and round nose pliers.

First, prepare a normal string or yarn with the same length that you want your bracelet to be. This is going to be the basis of how many hearts and jump rings you will use.

Second, cut a few wire pieces of that are 1.5 inches in length.

Third, with the wire held horizontally in front of you, clip the tip of the pliers a few centimeters from one end of the short wire and curl inwards. Do this to the other end of the wire.

Fourth, clip the tip of the pliers on the center of the wire and use your fingers to push each curled end towards each other. Make sure that they actually touch. This will be the wire hearts. Make more of them as you deem fit.

Fifth, connect the hearts with a jump ring between each heart. You can use one or two jump rings if you want. Make sure that each end of the necklace ends in one jump ring.

Sixth, if the chain has reached your desired length, set it aside and make your own hook and catch (as what you have learned in the previous chapter).

Finally, attach one end with the hook and the other with the catch. Now you have your own Chain of Hearts.

Project #4: Green is Love (Multi-strand Bead Bracelet)

You will need the following: stringing medium of your choice, normal string or yarn, 5 kinds of beads of your choice (can be of different sizes; should be green but of different shade for each kind), 18 gauge jewelry wire (silver), 2 eye pins, 2 jump rings, and 2 bead cones.

First, prepare a normal string or yarn with the same length that you want your bracelet to be. This is going to be the basis of how long your bracelet should be.

Second, cut up pieces of your stringing medium of the same length as the yarn or string, plus a few inches.

Third, get a jump ring and attach on it one end of each cut up stringing medium using crimp beads.

Fourth, string on the beads onto each stringing medium, then attach and secure the other ends on another jump ring using crimp beads.

Fifth, attach an eye pin on each jump ring. Take the bead cones and inert them through the other end of the eye pin. If the hole on the bead cone is larger, string one small round bead before and after beading cone. Make a wrapped loop using the extra part of the eye pins.

Sixth, make your own hook and catch. And finally, attach one end with the hook and the other with the catch. Now you have your own multi-strand Green is Love bracelet.

Printed in Great Britain
by Amazon

73666250R00024